"Hey Ranger!"

Kids Ask Questions About
Rocky Mountain National Park

Kim Williams Justesen

Illustrated by Judy Newhouse

FALCONGUIDE®

GUILFORD, CONNECTICUT
HELENA, MONTANA
AN IMPRINT OF THE GLOBE PEQUOT PRESS

With special thanks to Morgan, Ryan, and Amanda—three of the greatest kids on earth, and to Mike, my incredible husband. Your love and support are what makes this dream possible. Thanks also to the many dedicated and awesome rangers in the National Park Service. You are all truly national treasures.

Copyright © 2006 by Morris Book Publishing, LLC.

Falcon and FalconGuide are registered trademarks of Morris Book Publishing, LLC.

Illustrations by Judy Newhouse © Morris Book Publishing, LLC.

Library of Congress Cataloging-in-Publication Data is available.
ISBN 0-7627-3848-0

Manufactured in the United States of America
First Edition/First Printing

To buy books in quantity for corporate use
or incentives, call **(800) 962–0973, ext. 4551,**
or e-mail **premiums@GlobePequot.com.**

Introduction

Every year millions of people visit America's national parks. They come to see the many different natural wonders across our land and to learn more about what makes our country unique. Thousands of park rangers help visitors from around the world understand and enjoy all the great sights in our parks. They manage the resources of the parks, keep visitors safe, and answer tourists' questions.

No matter if the question is great or goofy, the ranger's job is to treat each guest with respect and to handle each question with a straight face. Rangers have heard it all, but they stay friendly and helpful, even if they have answered the same question one hundred times or more that day.

Rangers live in the parks where they work, so when they talk about the park, they are also talking about their home. Rangers live and work in the national parks, but the parks belong to the American people. These lands were set aside to protect their unique natural environments.

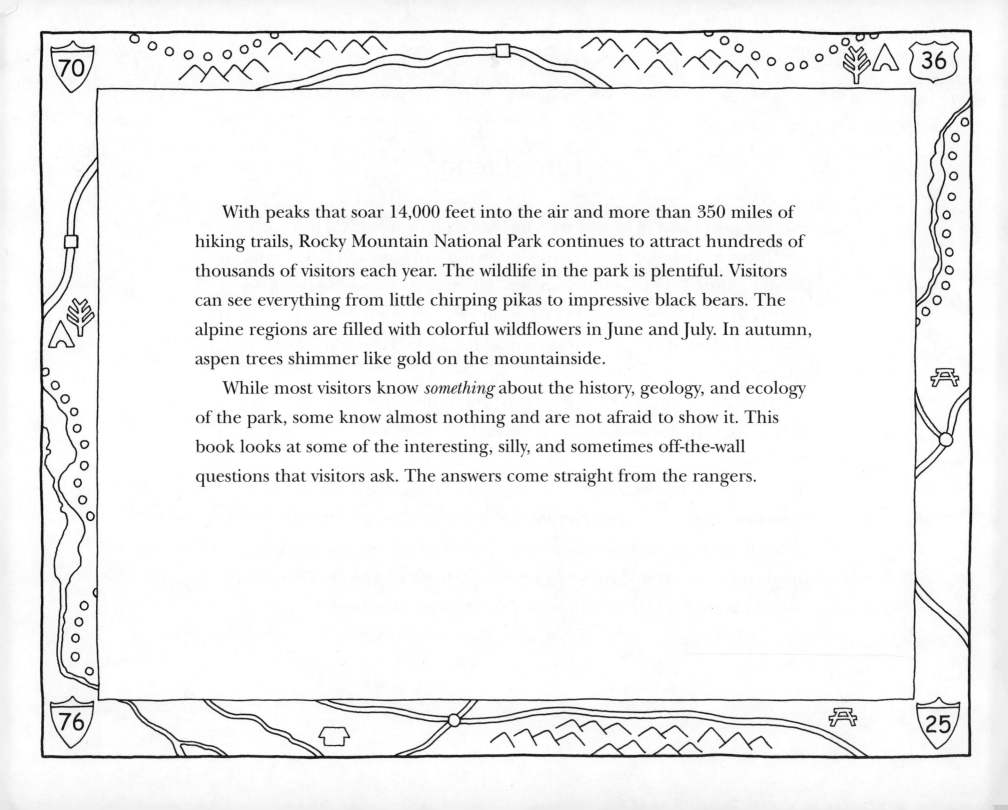

With peaks that soar 14,000 feet into the air and more than 350 miles of hiking trails, Rocky Mountain National Park continues to attract hundreds of thousands of visitors each year. The wildlife in the park is plentiful. Visitors can see everything from little chirping pikas to impressive black bears. The alpine regions are filled with colorful wildflowers in June and July. In autumn, aspen trees shimmer like gold on the mountainside.

While most visitors know *something* about the history, geology, and ecology of the park, some know almost nothing and are not afraid to show it. This book looks at some of the interesting, silly, and sometimes off-the-wall questions that visitors ask. The answers come straight from the rangers.

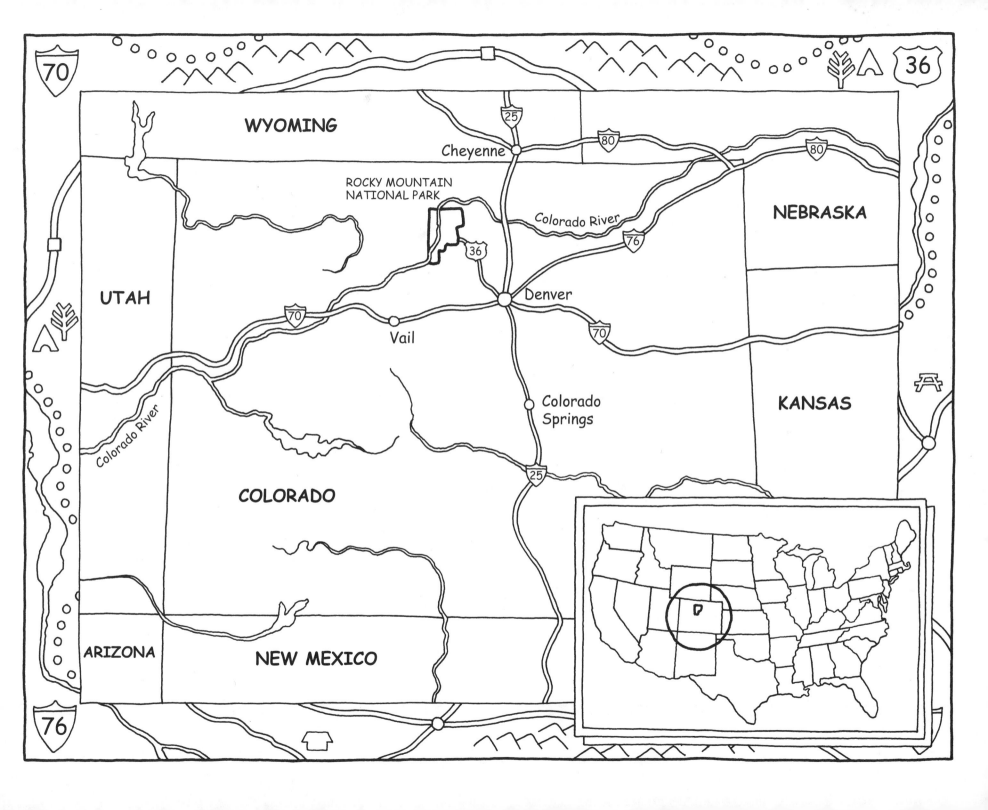

Who discovered Rocky Mountain National Park?

Around 11,000 years ago humans first made their way into the valleys and meadows that now make up Rocky Mountain National Park. For thousands of years Native Americans made seasonal visits to these beautiful mountains. Researchers have found broken spearheads and hide-scrapers along what are thought to be the trails used by these nomadic peoples. Eventually this area became the favorite summer hunting grounds of the Ute people.

In the early 1800s French trappers and Spanish explorers came close to today's park boundaries, but the spectacular scenes within the park remained hidden from European eyes. Explorers other than Native Americans did not find a way past the towering peaks to see the wonders of Rocky Mountain until the mid-1850s.

Who is Joel Estes?
Why does he have his own park?

Joel Estes, for whom Estes Park, Colorado, is named, was born in Kentucky in the early 1800s. While he and his son were scouting for game one autumn, they climbed a small peak that overlooked a valley of such beauty that the elder Estes decided to make it his home. In 1860 his family settled into the area that now bears his name. After just six years, however, the Estes family found the conditions too harsh, and they sold their cabin for a yoke of oxen. The new owners turned the cabin into a hotel of sorts, and visitors have been coming ever since.

While Estes's former home is still called Estes Park, it is not itself a national park. Many people are confused by name and by the fact that Estes Park is one of the gateways to Rocky Mountain National Park.

Who was Longs Peak named for?

Longs Peak was named after Stephen H. Long, an early nineteenth-century explorer. He brought explorers close to the area of the park, but they got no closer than 40 miles to the mountain that now bears his name.

Longs Peak towers above the park, reaching to 14,259 feet. Its craggy face shows the scars of the hard weather that can strike year-round. Snow on the peak is often visible to park visitors even during the hot summer months.

The first known person to climb to the top of Longs Peak was the great explorer John Wesley Powell. He reached the top in 1868. In 1873 Anna Dickinson became the first woman to achieve this same goal.

Why aren't there more paths and walkways at Rocky Mountain National Park?

Rocky Mountain boasts more than 350 miles of paths throughout the 265,828 acres of the park. Many of these trails are easy for anyone to use, but some are more challenging and some require backcountry permits. These permits tell rangers who you are, where you are going, how long you intend to be there, and who is going with you. All this is important information, because the backcountry can be a dangerous place.

The National Park Service is very careful about where it places paths and walkways. It has to consider the safety of the visitors, the safety of the wildlife, and the impact the path and visitors will have on the ecosystem.

Rocky Mountain National Park is a wilderness. It is nature at its most wild, and that can mean a lot of dangers. Elk, bears, porcupines, and badgers are common in the park. These animals will attack humans if they feel threatened or are frightened by an unexpected hiker. Each year rangers treat dozens of injuries caused by the unexpected encounter between man and animal.

Are there trams or buses in the park?

In some areas of the park, there are. On the Bear Lake Road, between trailheads up to the Glacier Park Campground and up to Moraine Park over to Cub Lake and Fern Lake, you can ride in comfort, enjoy the sights, and not worry about traffic. The shuttle buses are offered as a convenience at Rocky Mountain. The buses are intended to help reduce the risk of damage from pollution, garbage, and large numbers of visitors.

Who owns all the great buildings and houses? Can I build my house here, too?

Rangers and park employees use most of the houses and buildings around the park as living quarters while they work in the park. There are a few concession buildings and one privately owned home within the park boundaries. The private home was built through a special agreement with the Park Service many years ago. The National Park Service no longer offers private-home permits, so even though the park belongs to the American people, you can't build your home here.

We waited all winter to drive the Trail Ridge Road. Then when we did, we got sick! Why?

One of the best parts of Rocky Mountain is the chance to see breathtaking mountain vistas that you cannot see anywhere else. To experience some of the most spectacular views, a trip along the Trail Ridge Road is the best route.

It is important to remember, however, that this road reaches an elevation of more than 12,000 feet—that's about 2½ miles up into the atmosphere. If you are not used to high elevations such as this, you may feel ill. Many park visitors who come from lower-lying areas experience altitude sickness. If you feel dizzy, nauseous, and short of breath, or experience a headache or ringing in the ears, you might be experiencing altitude sickness. The best thing you can do is get to a lower area and wait for your body to return to normal. In extreme cases seek medical attention.

When is the Trail Ridge Road open?
Every time we come, it's closed.

Because of its rough terrain and elevation, the Trail Ridge Road is often closed because of snow. Typically the road opens in May and closes in October. That leaves only the months of June, July, August, and September for park visitors to take advantage of the views.

Plowing to open the road begins in mid-April each year. It typically takes forty-two days to plow enough of the snow to open the road. But it can take even longer. Some years it has taken as many as fifty-five days—that's nearly two months—to clear the road for visitors.

Rocky Mountain can receive as many as 250 to 300 inches of snow each year. Plowing that much snow takes a special kind of snowplow. The rotary plow can cut into snowdrifts as high as 21 feet. The blower connected to the rotary can shoot snow up to 150 feet away from the plow.

People in Colorado must be used to snow. Why can't they keep Trail Ridge Road open year-round?

Even with special equipment, it takes a lot of time, people, and money to keep snow off Trail Ridge Road. The equipment must be fueled, oiled, and greased each morning. The cost to open just Trail Ridge Road can be more than $36,000 per year. Besides the costs, travel on the road is dangerous during the winter months. Blowing snow, high winds, blinding snowfall, and icy conditions make travel unsafe for cars and trucks.

With weather this bad, how could anybody survive?

The weather is a challenge, and it certainly made life difficult for the early settlers in the area. The grazing season was too short to keep cattle, the growing season was too short to raise crops, and the winter storms could make temperatures almost unlivable. Many early settlers left during the winter months, but those who stayed had to spend the summer bringing in loads and loads of food, warm clothing, and wood for cooking and heating.

Where is the museum?

There isn't a museum in the traditional sense, but Rocky Mountain has a museum storage facility. It is located behind the Beaver Meadows Visitor Center and holds tens of thousands of items related to the park's natural history, cultural history, and archives. You can tour this building and see some of the amazing artifacts that have been discovered and donated over the years. There are spear points and arrowheads left behind by Native Americans, antique furniture from the cabins of early settlers, china used at one of the first lodges opened within the park, and thousands of lantern slides.

Where can I find the Heart of the Rockies?

That all depends on what you're looking for. A few western states, such as Wyoming, Montana, Utah, and Colorado, claim that title. Or you can find the Heart of the Rockies online. Heart of the Rockies is an educational program for teachers and schools to help teach kids about nature, the environment, and Rocky Mountain. If you visit www.HeartoftheRockies.net, you can play games and even become a Web Ranger.™

Why can't we feed or ride the animals?
They look so gentle and cute.

While the animals *look* tame, they are still wild animals, and even the nicest ones will attack humans if the animal feels threatened. Elk can charge at speeds up to 50 miles per hour. They have been known to knock visitors over with their large antlers and kick them with their strong hooves. Moose will also knock over people and stomp on them if they get too close. They also have been known to kill people with their powerful legs.

Bighorn sheep have those huge, tough horns that are curled back to protect their skulls when they butt into a challenger or other threat. Badgers have sharp teeth like razors, as do wolverines. Even cute little chipmunks and mice can bite through skin. They can also carry diseases that are dangerous to humans. When you see animals in the park, stay in your car. If you are hiking, move away slowly to a safe distance. Park rangers recommend keeping at least 100 yards away from large animals like elk or moose. You should keep even further away from bears.

What time do you let the animals out for feeding?

Some people think that national parks are like zoos. The truth is, when you visit Rocky Mountain National Park, you are visiting the animals in their natural habitat. They are not kept in cages. They eat as animals do in nature. The best time to see animals eating is early in the morning before sunrise, or at dusk as the sun is setting. A ranger can tell you where different animals have been seen enjoying a meal.

Why do you let so many wild animals run loose in the park?

For the same reason why the animals are not fed on a schedule. They live in Rocky Mountain National Park. Unlike a zoo, where animals are kept in cages or restricted areas, the animals here are wild and live in the wilderness. This area is the natural home to bears, moose, deer, eagles, elk, raccoons, skunks, chipmunks, squirrels, and many other animals. When you visit Rocky Mountain, you are visiting these amazing creatures in their home, and we need to treat their home with respect.

What about the bears? Can we feed them?

For a long time feeding the bears was considered part of the fun of visiting a national park. People would feed bears bread, marshmallows, or other food from their car windows. Brave souls would get out of their cars and feed the bears by hand. Unfortunately, this led to many injuries by hungry and aggressive bears. It also led to unhealthy, uncooperative bears. After many years of being fed by humans, raiding park garbage dumps, and learning to be dependent on people for food, the bears had become more and more aggressive with people and were showing signs of poor health and many illnesses.

Scientists and rangers now know that bears need protein from animal meat and wild berries and nuts. Hunting and killing their own food also helps keep bears healthy and keeps them from being tempted by human food. When bears begin relying on human food, they become a problem and have to be moved farther away from humans. If that doesn't work, they have to be put to sleep by rangers and veterinarians.

How old are deer when they turn into elk?

Although they look alike, deer and elk are two different animals. They do have some things in common, however. They both have antlers and their body type is similar. But elk are bigger than deer, and elk make a distinctive sound called bugling, which sounds like a trumpet blowing. Elk antlers are large with broad flat parts rimmed with little pointy spines. Deer have smaller antlers that grow in long slender spikes.

How high up do you have to go before the deer turn into elk?

The basis of this question might be the misconception that elk live at a higher elevation than deer live. Actually you can find both mule deer and elk living side by side at all different elevations throughout the park. Because deer and elk are strong, hearty animals, the altitude does not affect them. Their hearts and lungs are well adapted to living in the thinner air of the higher elevations.

When do horns turn into antlers?

There is a difference between horns and antlers. Horns, like those on bighorn sheep, are permanent. They stay attached to the animal's skull even when they die. Horns are made out of keratin, which is a type of protein. It's the same stuff that makes up fingernails. Antlers, like those on mule deer, are made of a mineral called calcium carbonate. This is the same stuff that makes up human bones.

Why do you take the antlers off the elk?

Unlike horns, antlers are not permanent. They fall off each year in the spring and grow back over the year. In the fall, elk use their antlers as part of their mating ritual. They rattle their antlers together like swords as a way to intimidate other bull elk (males) and to attract cow elk (females).

If an elk becomes too aggressive, the park rangers may have to remove its antlers. The elk is given medicine to make it sleepy. Then the ranger carefully cuts the antlers down to just a few inches so that the animal can't hurt anyone or do any damage to cars or signs.

Why can't I get out of my car to take pictures of the animals?

Most every animal in the park is faster than you are, and quite a few of them are stronger. Taking pictures is fine if you pull your car over in a turnout, and if you observe the rules on keeping a safe distance from the animals. If you want a picture of a bear, for example, you should stay in your car or use a telephoto lens on your camera. You should never be closer than 200 yards to a bear, no matter what. If rangers ask you to stay in your car, or to get back in your car while you're looking at animals, you should definitely do it.

What animals are here that we can't see?

Moose are often hard to see, because they are somewhat reclusive animals that prefer swampy, wet areas. They also live in smaller groups than elk and deer do. Beavers are difficult to see, because they do their work in streams and creeks. They also tend to stay away from humans. Badgers and wolverines are hard to find, because they like the shelter of the deep woods. There are bats that come out only at night. Owls sleep during the day, too. It takes sharp eyes to see some of the animals, but park rangers can tell you the best places to look.

How do you get the trees planted so evenly?

Rangers do not come in and plant trees, and they don't hire anyone to do it either. That's what makes Rocky Mountain so beautiful—it's all done by nature.

When a tree reseeds, it needs good soil, sunlight, and water. To get enough of each of these things, there has to be enough space between the new tree and other trees or plants around it. If the seed lands in the shadow of another tree, it doesn't stand as much chance of growing big. Animals, such as squirrels, mice, and birds, also spread seeds. This gives new trees a better chance of getting that sunshine and water they need.

What kills the trees?
Why don't the rangers stop it?

Lightning kills some trees. Others die of old age. Falling rocks, heavy snow, or even avalanches can destroy trees, too. A forest can be infested with bugs that bore into the core of the trees, killing them from the inside out. There isn't much that rangers can do to prevent the loss of trees. It is just part of the natural cycle in the forest.

Why don't you take out the dead trees in the forest?

As with most things in our national parks, Mother Nature does the best job of management.

Some of the dead trees were killed by fire. Others may have been struck by lightning. Dead trees that remain standing, even though they are burned and hollow, provide homes for animals such as bats and squirrels, insects, and small rodents. They are part of the natural state of the Rocky Mountain forest.

In time the trees will fall on their own. Wind, snow, or even rain-soaked ground will help the trees to topple. Once down, the trees will begin to decay, providing food for some insects and animals, as well as nourishment for the soil. This helps other trees and plants to grow, continuing the cycle of nature.

Why can't I pick flowers?

Lots of interesting and beautiful flowers grow in Rocky Mountain National Park. Penstemon grows in the wet, marshy areas. In the subalpine areas you'll see fairy slipper and twinflower. Queen's crown, snow buttercup, blue columbine, and alpine paintbrush grow in the alpine regions. However, with millions of visitors each year, imagine what would happen to Rocky Mountain if everyone took something, even just a few flowers. We would not have those flowers to look at, and over time the park would be stripped bare.

In addition, elk, moose, deer, and porcupines eat many of the plants and flowers that grow here. If too many visitors picked flowers in the park, it could lead to a shortage of food for the animals.

About Park Rangers

Park rangers come in all ages, colors, shapes, and sizes. They are men and women who care about our environment and enjoy working with people. Rangers do a lot in our parks. They provide information, give campfire talks on special topics, lead visitors on guided hikes, and oversee the day-to-day operations of parks. They also gather scientific information and create informational resources such as brochures and signs.

For guests who have a problem, such as a car accident or having something stolen, park rangers are like police officers. They take reports, help manage traffic, work like detectives, and even arrest people and hold them for the local police to pick up.

Park rangers help keep visitors safe and protect the wildlife and the environment in the park. They help fight forest fires, supervise campgrounds, find firewood for campers, and make sure that campers follow safe camping rules.

Rangers also lead the Junior Rangers Program, which gives kids a chance to learn more about the place they are visiting and more about what rangers do.

Rangers work in national parks, but they work at national historic sites, national forests, and at national monuments, too. They work in cities and in forests, at seashores and in historic buildings, at battlefields and archaeological sites, and at lakes and recreation areas. Rangers also might have to move a lot or live far from their families.

Rangers go to college to learn to do what they do. They study natural resource management, earth sciences, history, archaeology, anthropology, park and recreational management, law enforcement, social sciences, museum sciences, business, and other subjects. Once they become park rangers, they take more classes to learn about the place where they will be working, how to do their job better, and how to work with people.

Because many rangers work outside, they have to be in good physical shape. While leading a guided trail walk or checking on the condition of a trail, rangers can hike up to 15 miles or more a day.

No matter where they work, rangers share a love of their job, a concern for the safety of visitors, an appreciation for the resources they protect, and a respect for the special country that is home to so many wonderful places.

NATIONAL
PARK
SERVICE

About the Author

Kim Williams Justesen lives with her husband, three children, two cats, and one dog in their home in Sandy, Utah. Kim earned her bachelor's degree in English from Westminster College of Salt Lake City and her masters in writing for children from Vermont College in Montpelier. Besides camping and hiking in our national parks, Kim enjoys knitting, crocheting, and reading. In addition to writing, she teaches English at a small, private college in Salt Lake City.

About the Artist

Illustrator Judy Newhouse is a graduate of Moore College of Art in Pennsylvania. Her work ranges from cartoons to precise medical drawings. She lives with her artist husband in a log house in Chester Springs, Pennsylvania. When not illustrating books, Judy loves to garden, cook, travel, and visit her daughter, an actor in New York City.